Keith W

Kagiso's Mad Uncle

Illustrated by
Robert Geary

HEINEMANN

Heinemann International Literature and Textbooks
a division of Heinemann Educational Books Ltd
Halley Court, Jordan Hill, Oxford OX2 8EJ

Heinemann Educational Boleswa
PO Box 10103, Village Post Office, Gaborone, Botswana
Heinemann Educational Books (Nigeria) Ltd
PMB 5205, Ibadan
Heinemann Kenya Ltd
Kijabe Street, PO Box 45314, Nairobi

LONDON EDINBURGH PARIS MADRID
ATHENS BOLOGNA MELBOURNE
SYDNEY AUCKLAND PORTSMOUTH (NH)
SINGAPORE TOKYO HARARE

First published by Heinemann International Literature and Textbooks in 1991

British Library Cataloguing in Publication Data
Whiteley, Keith
Kagiso's mad uncle
I. Title II. Series
823.914 [J]

ISBN 0-435-89164-2

Illustrated by Robert Geary

Glossary
Difficult words are listed alphabetically on page 29

Printed and bound in Great Britain by
George Over Limited, Rugby and London
91 92 93 94 10 9 8 7 6 5 4 3 2 1

It was the very last day of the school year. The class teacher was reading out a list of names. It was the names of the pupils who had done well in their final primary school exams.

'Beauty Sibisi, Bernard Silabo, Kagiso Tsima...'

Those children whose names had been called out were smiling. But Kagiso was not smiling.

Later, Bernard and Kagiso walked home together.

'I'm so excited,' said Bernard. 'Ma and Pa will be so pleased!'

Bernard's father was a government driver and his mother was a secretary.

Bernard jumped over the low wall into the well brushed compound around his home.

'Goodbye,' he shouted to his friend.

Kagiso walked sadly towards his own untidy hut where his father and brother were waiting for him.

‘Right,’ said Kagiso’s father as soon as Kagiso got home. ‘That’s school finished. Now it’s time for you to start work.’

‘Yes,’ agreed Pule, Kagiso’s older brother. ‘That’s right. Now it’s time for you to...’

‘But dad,’ said Kagiso, ‘I’ve done well in my exams. I can now go to secondary school.’

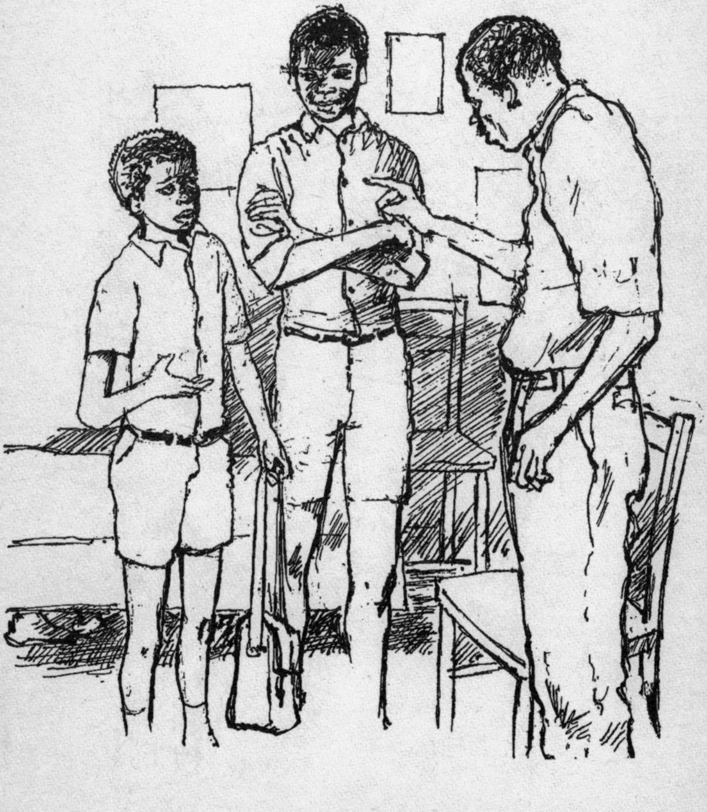

'Secondary school!' shouted Mr Tsima. He gave his son a smack on the ear. 'Don't talk to me about secondary school. You've had enough of school.'

'That's right,' laughed Pule. 'You've had enough of...'

'And I've had enough of you,' said Mr Tsima, giving Pule a smack as well.

'But dad...' Kagiso said again.

'Now what is it?'

'But didn't my mother want me to go to secondary school?'

Mr Tsima became very angry. He hit Kagiso again.

'Don't talk to me about your mother!' he shouted. 'I was wrong to marry her. She had too much education. Too much education makes you crazy. Your mother's family had too much education. Look at her brother - your uncle. She thought he was clever. But he's mad, completely mad!'

Kagiso's father never listened to him. Kagiso went to his own corner of the hut and lay down. He was only twelve years old, but he felt his life was finished.

Kagiso lay in the dark thinking about his mother. She had died when he was very young. He tried to remember what she had been like. She must have been beautiful. He was not able to remember her face, but he remembered her voice and sweet, sad smile. She had been kind to everyone. His father had been kinder then.

Kagiso remembered the day he started school. His mother had been educated, not like his father. She had understood English. She had helped him with his first sentences in English.

'Good Morning, mother.'

'How are you, my son?'

'I am well, thank you.'

'Today the sun is shining.'

But then, suddenly, she had died. Nearly six years ago. She had died and everything had changed. Kagiso wiped away tears from his eyes.

Then Kagiso thought about his uncle. Was he really mad? Once Kagiso had found an old envelope addressed to his mother, Mrs Naledi Tsima. The sender's address had been written on the back: Mr Mosele Motswagae,
Ramantsima Mental Hospital,
P O Box 127, Ramantsima.

Kagiso had taken the envelope to school. He had shown it to his teacher and asked her what a mental hospital was.

'Well, you know what a hospital is, Kagiso?'

'Yes, it's like St Joseph's. That's where my mother went when she was sick,' Kagiso said.

'That's right. Well, a mental hospital is where people go who are sick in the mind.'

'Do you mean - mad people?'

'That's what some people call them, Kagiso.'

So perhaps his father was right. His mother and his uncle were educated people. But she was dead and he was mad. Perhaps going to secondary school really was dangerous.

But true or not, Kagiso didn't find out. For in the new year, when Bernard and his other friends went to secondary school, Kagiso went off alone to the cattle post. There he stayed for a whole year. And there, every day, in sun and in rain, he thought and thought.

Sometimes, at weekends, his friend Bernard visited Kagiso at the cattle post. He tried to tell Kagiso what he had learnt at school. And, sometimes, Bernard lent him his books.

Kagiso read about distant lands. He studied diagrams of plants and trees. He tried to remember all their names.

Kagiso also tried to study maths. He drew triangles and circles in the dust.

But one day, his father and his brother visited him unexpectedly.

'What are you doing?' his father shouted.

'Yes, what are you doing?' shouted Pule.

'Be quiet, you fool!' said Mr Tsima. Then he looked at the triangles and circles on the ground. He stamped angrily with his foot and covered the drawings and the young boy with dust.

'I've told you, boy,' shouted Mr Tsima, 'no more studying for you.'

After Kagiso's father had gone, the young boy kicked dust over his spoiled drawings.

'It's better to have a mad uncle than a cruel father and a stupid brother,' he thought to himself. 'I must escape from this terrible life.'

That night he made a plan.

There were days when Kagiso did not have to work and Pule looked after the cattle. On those days Kagiso went to the houses where the teachers lived. School pupils were not allowed to visit the teachers' houses or ask for work. But Kagiso was not a pupil, so he was able to do odd jobs like washing cars, tidying gardens or running errands. All the money he got, he gave to Bernard. Bernard kept the money safely in his house. He knew what his friend was planning.

At last, Kagiso was ready. One morning he left home early, as he always did when he was going to the cattle post. But this morning he didn't go to the cattle post. He went quietly to Bernard's house.

Kagiso picked up some small stones. He threw them at the window nearest to where Bernard slept. Silence! A long time passed. It was dark and Kagiso shivered with cold.

At last Kagiso heard a sleepy voice.

'Good luck!' the voice called.

There was a noise of something hitting the ground. Kagiso jumped over the wall and picked up an old grey sock. The money he had saved was hidden in a chocolate wrapper, inside the sock.

As Kagiso walked to the bus stop, the sun was rising.

It was a long journey. Kagiso had to change buses twice to get to Ramantsima. On each bus, he squeezed himself into a corner. He did not want to be noticed. Around him people were talking and laughing. The bus conductor pushed through the passengers, collecting fares and joking with all the young girls.

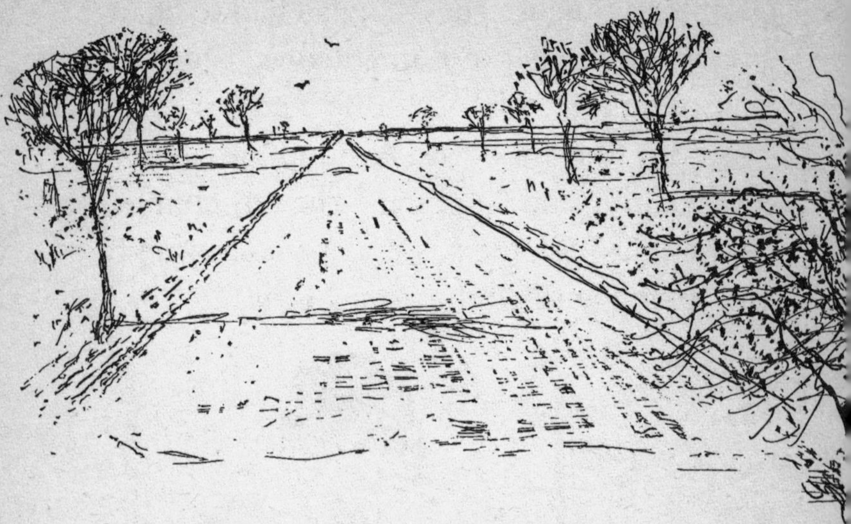

As the bus drove along Kagiso thought about his uncle. Was he really mad? Perhaps he really was dangerous!

The bus stopped suddenly.

'Ramantsima!' shouted the bus conductor.

Kagiso climbed down and the bus went on. He was left alone. It was now early afternoon, and he was hungry. He bought some fat-cakes and a Fanta at a stall. Now he had no money left.

'Excuse me, madam. How do I get to Ramantsima hospital?' he asked the stallholder politely.

'Hospital?' The stallholder thought for a moment or two. 'The nearest hospital's twenty kilometres away... Ah, you mean the mad house on the hill! Go on up the hill for about three kilometres. Then, you'll see a big, white building. That's what you're looking for. But be careful!'

Three kilometres! The sun was strong and Kagiso walked slowly. He wasn't sure if he really wanted to get there, but it was too late now. He had no money for the journey back home.

Then, suddenly, there it was - 'Ramantsima Mental Hospital'.

Kagiso took a deep breath. He walked through the gates and up a path. On each side of him there were flowering bushes and in front of him was a well-dressed family. But where was his uncle?

Kagiso came to the front door. The people in front of him walked in, so he followed them. They spoke to a young woman in a white uniform. Then they went through another door. Kagiso turned to speak to the young woman too, but she had gone.

Kagiso was lost. There were people walking about everywhere - men and women. Some were wearing white coats, some were wearing ordinary clothes.

Where were all the mad people?

Suddenly a big, wild-eyed man came walking quickly towards him. Kagiso jumped out of the way. A nurse was running.

'Mr Motswagae! Mr Motswagae!' she called.

Then she stopped and shook her head. 'Oh dear, he's in a very bad mood today,' she said out loud.

Kagiso had seen his uncle at last. The man was really mad. Perhaps he was dangerous. Why was he wearing a white coat?

Kagiso turned and walked back to the front door. Tears were running down his cheeks. He had lost all hope.

'What's the matter with you?' asked the nurse who had been following his uncle.

'Leave me alone,' said Kagiso. 'I've seen him now. Father was right. He is mad - really mad.'

'Who are you talking about?' asked the nurse.

'The big man in the white coat. He's my uncle. I hoped he wasn't mad. I hoped...'

'Mr Motswagae? Your uncle?' said the nurse, in surprise. 'Stop that crying and come with me.'

Mosele Motswagae sat behind his huge desk. He looked at the small boy sitting on the chair in front of him.

'So you're Naledi's younger boy,' he said.

'I thought you were mad,' said Kagiso in surprise.

'What! Me? I'm not mad.' And his uncle passed a packet of paper handkerchiefs across the desk. 'Here, blow your nose, boy.'

'But... you're not a doctor, are you? The nurse called you Mister.'

'Well, I am a doctor, but they don't call me doctor. I'm a specialist and specialists are called Mister.'

Kagiso did not understand.

'But... the nurse... she said you were in a very bad mood today.'

'What! She did, did she?' said Motwagae. Then he laughed, 'sometimes I get angry and lose my temper. But I'm not mad.'

At that moment, the nurse brought in a tray with a plate of biscuits and a glass of orange.

'Now drink up and eat those biscuits,' said Mr Motswagae. 'Then tell me why you've come to visit me.'

So Kagiso told his story.

'... and I thought you were mad, you see,' he ended.

Mr Motswagae spoke quietly, to himself. 'Why didn't I do more to help Mr Tsima. He was very upset when my sister, Naledi, died. I wrote once, but he never replied. Perhaps I was mad. I spend my life helping other people, but I didn't try to help my sister's family. Now I must do something to help them.'

Mr Motswagae looked at Kagiso. 'We must let your father know you're safe,' he said. 'He'll be very worried about you.'

'I was wrong to run away,' said Kagiso. 'But I do want to go to school.'

'I have an idea,' said Kagiso's uncle. 'Perhaps you can go to school here, eh? You can stay with me during term and go home for the holidays.'

Kagiso smiled.

'My uncle isn't mad!' he thought to himself. 'He's a very clever man.'

Questions

1 Who is Bernard?
2 How old was Kagiso when his mother died? How old is he at the start of the story?
3 Why did Kagiso think his uncle was mad?
4 How did Bernard help Kagiso to study?
5 How did Kagiso make some extra money?
6 What made Kagiso sure his uncle was mad, when he arrived at the hospital?
7 Why wasn't Mr Motswagae called Dr Motswagae?
8 'I have an idea,' said Mr Motswagae. What was Mr Motswagae's idea?

Activities

1 Draw pictures of Bernard's house and Kagiso's house. Show how they are different.
2 Imagine you are Kagiso, sitting alone at the cattle post. Write a letter to a friend describing how you feel.
3 Have you ever gone on a long journey alone? Describe your longest journey to a friend. Draw a map of where you went.
4 Mr Tsima says: 'Education makes you crazy.' Is he right or wrong? Have a class debate or talk about this with a friend.

Glossary

cruel (page 12) unkind
dangerous (page 10) something which does you harm is *dangerous*
errands - run errands (page 14) to go on short journeys for people, take messages and get things. Kagiso does this to make some pocket money
excited (page 2) feel strongly about something
fare (page 17) money paid for the bus journey
mood (page 22) how you feel. To be *in a bad mood* is to feel angry
smack (page 4) a hard hit
specialist (page 24) a doctor who knows a lot about one particular illness
spoiled (page 12) broken up and destroyed
squeeze (page 17) to press tightly
stamp (page 12) to put your foot down hard
stallholder (page 18) a person who has a small stall or open-air shop
unexpectedly (page 11) without warning
uniform (page 21) special clothes worn by people for their job, eg doctor, nurse, school pupil, etc
upset (page 27) very sad and unhappy
wipe (page 7) to rub away
worried (page 27) feel unhappy
wrapper (page 16) a paper cover

The Junior African Writers Series is designed to provide interesting and varied African stories either for pleasure or for study. There are four graded levels in the series.

Level 2 is for readers who have reached an elementary stage in English. The content and language have been carefully controlled to increase fluency in reading.

Content: The plots are straightforward and the number of characters is kept to a minimum. The information is presented in manageable amounts and the illustrations clarify the text.

Language: Reading is a learning experience and although the choice of words is carefully controlled (basic vocabulary level of about 800 words), new words, important to the story, are also introduced. These are contextualised, recycled through the story and explained in the glossary. The sentences are short and simple with a maximum of two clauses.

Glossary: Difficult words which students may not know and which are not made clear in the illustrations have been listed alphabetically at the back of the book. The definitions refer to the way the word is used in the story and the page reference is for the word's first use.

Questions and Activities: The questions give useful comprehension practice and ensure that the reader has followed and understood the story. The activities develop themes and ideas introduced and can be done as pairwork or groupwork in class, or as homework.

Other JAWS titles at Level 2

Masquerade Time, Cyprian Ekwensi, 0 435 89165 0
The Magic Pool, Gaele Mogwe, 0 435 89166 9